# Justice League

## Snyder's Recipes

## Luke Sack

# License Notes

The author of this book does not give permission to reproduce this material in print, electronic copies, photocopies or in whole or in part by social media, or in any other form. Permission must be given in writing for any exceptions.

The author of this book has taken every precaution to ensure the contents are accurate but accepts no responsibility for any damages that may occur as a result of following the material. The reader assumes all risk when following the content and is responsible for any costs associated with damages.

# Table of Contents

# Introduction

What do superheroes eat? And what do superheroes fans eat while watching their superheroes play their roles in their favorite movie? Well, in this recipe book, we will present amazing, delicious, and easy-to-make dishes that will not take you away from the Justice League.

# Superman's Herbal Butter T-Bone Steak

What do you give a big man for dinner? We love steak, and this is delicious.

**Cook time 70 minutes**

**Serves 2**

## Ingredients

- 2 well-trimmed t-bone steaks
- 1-stick of unsalted butter
- 1 tbsp chopped rosemary
- 1 tbsp parsley
- 1 inch finely grated ginger
- 2 cloves of garlic grated
- 1 tsp smoked chili flakes
- 1 tbsp salt kosher
- 1 tbsp black pepper

## Method

Season the steak generously with salt and pepper.

Sear in a pan for 3-5 minutes on both sides.

Put the pan into the oven until required doneness.

Meanwhile, whisk the parsley, butter, rosemary, ginger, garlic, chili flakes, and a little salt until soft.

Freeze and slice.

Serve with the steak.

# Batman's Buffalo Wings

We love his wings, and these are a great way to represent them.

**Cook time 70 minutes**

**Serves 2**

**Ingredients**

- 12 chicken wings
- 1 tsp garlic powder
- 1 tsp chili flakes
- 1 tsp paprika
- 1 tsp cayenne
- 1 cup of flour
- 1 tbsp butter
- ½ tsp ginger powder
- 1 scotch bonnet pepper chopped
- 1 tsp sugar
- 1 tbsp sweet chili sauce
- 1 tbsp white vinegar
- 1 tsp garlic
- Salt and pepper
- Oil to fry

**Method**

Season the chicken with ginger powder, garlic powder, chili flakes, paprika, cayenne, salt, and pepper and set aside for 10 -15 minutes.

Remove, coat in flour, and double fry to increase its crisp.

Meanwhile, in a pan, add the butter, sauce, scotch bonnet pepper, and garlic.

Add the sugar, chili sauce, vinegar, and season.

Toss the wings to coat and serve.

# United we win chocolate cake

I don't care how many demons he fought in how many hells, he has never fought us united. A cake for victory – team Justice League.

**Cook time 70 minutes**

**Serves 12**

## Ingredients

- 4 cups gooey chocolate spread
- 1 stick of unsalted butter melted
- ½ cup olive oil
- 1 packet of chocolate cake mix
- 3 large eggs
- 200g cream cheese
- 1 ¼ cups powdered sugar
- ¼ cup Mexican cocoa powder
- 1 tsp vanilla extra

## Method

Preheat the oven and line an 8-inch round pan – set aside.

Melt the butter and oil together.

Add an egg to the cake mix with half the butter/oil mix to form the batter.

In another mixing bowl, whip the cheese, sugar, cocoa powder, vanilla, eggs, and remaining oil mix until light and fluffy.

Mix both batters together folding gently.

Pour and bake until done but slightly gooey.

Allow it to cool and smother it with the chocolate spread.

# Darkseid Blackened Fish Fillet

Darkseid is counting in the division to turn the world into the dust. Does he know that Superman is back, trying to unite the team for one last battle?

**Cook time 12 minutes**

**Serves 2**

## Ingredients

- 2 fish fillets – firm white fish of choice
- ½ tsp chili flakes
- ½ tsp smoked paprika
- ½ tsp lemon salt
- ½ tsp ginger-garlic powder
- 2 tbsp olive oil
- 1 tbsp butter
- Salt and black pepper
- ½ cup fish stock

## Method

Combine the dry ingredients in a bowl and coat the fish.

Add the fish fillet to a pan with the butter and oil.

Cook fish until black and firm.

Add a little fish stock, cover with a lid and cook for 2 -5 minutes.

Serves with avocado salsa.

# Aquaman Spicy Squid bowl

This is simple, light, and will have him gliding through the water effortlessly.

**Cook time 40 minutes**

**Serves 2**

## Ingredients

- 1 tbsp black peppercorns
- 1 tbsp Sichuan pepper
- 1 tsp salt
- 1 large squid cleaned and cut into pieces
- ½ cup corn flour
- ½ cup rice flour
- 1 tsp chopped garlic
- 1 large red chili chopped
- 1 tbsp scallions
- Oil for frying
- 1 lime for garnish

**Method**

Add the black pepper and Sichuan pepper to a pan and toast slightly.

Add to a dry mill with the salt and pulverize.

Sprinkle the dry mix spice over the squid, massaging gently to coat.

Mix the flour in a bowl with a little of the spice mix and coat the squid pieces, dusting off any extras.

Place them directly into the oil to crisp and brown, set them aside.

In a wok, add a tbsp oil, the garlic, and chili, sauté for 1 minute and add the fried squid.

Add a sprinkle of the spice mix and scallion, cook for 2 minutes.

Serve with lime juice.

# Flash No-Bake Energy Bar

If he is going to beat the speed of light, he needs a reliable energy source, and these are the best.

**Cook time 20**

**Make 2 dozens +**

## Ingredients

- 200g chopped seeded dates
- ½ cup Manuka honey
- ¼ cup coconut flakes
- 1 ½ cups dry old-fashioned oats
- 1 cup shelled & chopped pistachio nuts
- 1 tbsp ground flax seed
- 1 cup dried cranberries
- ¼ cup golden dried raisin
- 1/3 cup dark chocolate chip

## Method

Add all the ingredients to a bowl.

Mix well and form into balls.

Store in the refrigerator.

# Superman Kryptonite Matcha Yokan

Superman may be scared of green; this green is delicious and harmless.

**Cook time 20 minutes**

**Serves 4**

## Ingredients

### For the Matcha

- ½ tsp agar-agar
- 1 tsp Matcha tea
- 3 tbsp baker's sugar
- 50ml water

### For the Mizu

- ½ cup red bean paste
- ½ cup water
- 1 tsp Matcha powder

## Method

Add the agar-agar and water in a saucepan.

Add the sugar, Matcha, and stir under low heat until it's dissolved and consistent/ set aside.

Mix the water, paste, and Matcha in a bowl until its consistent.

Mix both mixtures together and pour into a silicone mold.

Allow it to set and cut into cubes.

Enjoy.

# Steppenwolf Butterfly chicken

His head looks like butterflied chicken, so why not. He is the main villain in Snyder's cut Justice League but has a boss this time.

**Cook time 60 minutes**

**Serves 6**

## Ingredients

- 1 -2.5kg bird
- 1 tbsp ginger/garlic paste
- 1 tbsp butter
- ½ tbsp chili flakes
- Salt and pepper

## Method

Butterfly the chicken by cutting away the spine.

Mix the spices in a bowl and rub them under the skin and on it.

Pay attention to the breast region.

Place into the oven and allow it to cook.

Serve as desired.

# Cyborg pan-fried fish Steak

We are pan-frying this in a pan because it's the same material type as Cyborg armor.

**Cook time 15 minutes**

**Serves 4**

## Ingredients

- 4 fish steaks cod or John Dory
- Salt and pepper
- 1 stick butter
- 2 garlic cloves crushed
- Half a lemon

## Method

Add a little butter to the pan.

Season the fish.

Place it skin-side into the pan and allow it to cook until skin is crisp.

Flip to the other side and add more butter and garlic as they cook.

Baste the fish with garlic butter and finish off with a squeeze of lemon.

Serve with a crunchy salad.

# A Tribute to Team

It's just like the team, all different but work together beautifully.

**Prep time 10 minutes**

**Makes a bowl**

## Ingredients

- 1 cup fresh chopped cilantro
- 2 limes juiced
- 1 large garlic clove grated
- 1 dash of cumin
- 1 (5-oz.) can corn drained
- 1 tsp smoked paprika
- ½ cup chopped Roma tomatoes
- 1 yellow, red, green, and orange color bell peppers diced
- 1 med purple onion chopped
- 1 cup canned black beans drained
- Salt and pepper to taste
- 1 jalapeño, chopped

## Method

Add the vegetables into a bowl.

Add the salt, pepper, and lime juice.

Allow it to sit for 5 to 10 minutes.

Serve when ready.

# A Flash Dish from Time – Croquettes

He makes the journey back in time to fix the wrong he caused and makes it just in time too.

**Cook time 60 minutes**

**Serves 4**

## Ingredients

- 4 cups cooked and mashed African Yams
- 1 red chili chopped
- 2 cups diced juice chicken thighs
- Salt and pepper
- 2 eggs beaten
- 2 cups panko crumbs
- 2 tbsp chopped onions
- Oil to fry
- 1 tsp garlic, ginger, and cumin each

## Method

Mix the yam, chili, chicken, onion, and spices in a bowl.

Season and form into balls.

Dip in egg, then crumbs and fry.

Serve as desired.

# Spartan's Skordalia

As the movie progresses, you see other heroes battling Darkseid and his cohorts, including Spartan.

**Cook time 30 minutes**

**Makes a bowl**

## Ingredients

- 8 cloves of roasted garlic
- 450g white potatoes
- 240ml fresh extra virgin olive oil
- ½ lemon, juiced
- Salt and black pepper

## Method

Cook potatoes until soft, drain, and pour into a mixer.

Add the garlic, and salt & pepper.

As its gentle spins, add the oil a tbsp at a time.

Add the lemon juice to taste.

Balance out the flavors and serve with extra olive oil.

# Martian huntsman corn cake

Guess that is what they eat, but this should be a good one.

**Cook time 80 minutes**

**Serves 10**

**Ingredients**

- 1 (500g) can corn
- 1 ½ cups evaporated milk
- 2 cups coarse cornmeal
- ½ cup sugar white
- ½ cup honey
- 1 tsp baking powder
- ½ cup butter
- ¼ cup oil
- 4 eggs
- 1 cup coconut flakes sweetened
- ¼ tsp salt

**Method**

Blend the canned corn and milk in a blend.

Add the cornmeal, sugar, honey, oil, melted butter, eggs, baking powder, and salt.

Pour the batter into two 8-inch pans and into a preheated oven.

Cook until a skewer comes out clean and cool before taking it out of the pan.

Serve.

# Steppenwolf Atlantic Fish sticks

This ruthless monster finds his way to Atlantis as he hunts for the three boxes on earth.

**Cook time 20 minutes**

**Serves 2**

**Ingredients**

- 1 cup buttermilk
- 2 large white fish fillets cut in 1-inch thick strips
- 2 cups panko crumbs or more
- 2 eggs beaten
- 1 tsp garlic and ginger powder
- Salt and pepper
- 1 tsp chili
- Oil for frying

**Method**

Season the fish with ginger, garlic, chili, salt and pepper, and soak in buttermilk for 10 minutes.

Coat in panko, dip in eggs, and in panko again.

Gently place into the hot oil to fry until crisp.

# Lois Veggie Rolls

She is a humble girl that fell in love with a superhero. So, what's for lunch?

**Prep time 15 minutes**

**Serves 2**

## Ingredients

- 2 tbsp homemade hummus
- 2 pita bread
- 2 carrots sliced into sticks
- 2 cucumbers seeded and cut in sticks
- 2 celery sticks, cut thinly
- A handful of cilantro chopped
- Salt and pepper
- Drizzle of honey for sweetness

## Method

Assemble the ingredients in the bread.

Drizzle with honey and wrap.

# Sweet & Spicy Over Roasted Carrot

This is a simple and delicious way for the heroes to snack during work hours.

**Cook time 60 minutes**

**Serves 4**

## Ingredients

- 2 pounds sweet carrot cut into sticks
- ¼ cup organic honey
- 1 tsp red chili chopped
- 2 sprigs thyme chopped
- Dash of salt
- 2 tbsp oil

## Method

Toss all the ingredients in a bowl.

Bake in the oven until it is soft but slightly brown and crunchy.

Allow it to cool down and serve.

# The Amazon Sweet Potato Kale Salad

For an Amazon queen to retain her ageless beauty, she must be eating right. If you love wonder woman, this is a simple recipe to try.

**Prep time 30 minutes**

**Serves 2**

**Ingredients**

- 2 cups sweet potatoes cubes
- 1 pack fresh spinach store-bought
- 1 tsp garlic
- Salt and pepper
- 1 tbsp butter
- 1 cup cooked brown rice or quinoa
- 2 tbsp Dijon-mayo dressing

**Method**

Add salt, pepper, garlic, and butter to the sweet potatoes.

Bake in the oven until soft but firm.

Add the rice to a bowl, spinach, and potatoes, toss with the dressing and serve.

# A Fruity vodka cocktail to ease the mind

Every superhero needs a drink at some point, even the Justice League too.

**Prep time 30 minutes**

**Serves 4**

**Ingredients**

- 250ml vodka
- 1-liter cranberry juice
- 500ml orange juice
- 1 cup fresh cranberries
- 4 lemon slices of decoration
- 4 thyme sprigs

**Method**

Mix the first three ingredients in a shaker.

Pour into a glass with ice.

Top with fresh cranberries & thyme.

Serve.

# On a date with Wonder woman

You think she will date younger boys; she is 5000 years old, every man is a younger boy, says Cyborg as they dug Superman's grave.

**Cook time 13 minutes**

**Serves 2**

**Ingredients**

- 1 dozen fresh oyster, cleaned in shells
- 1 lime
- 1 small shallot chopped
- 1 tsp garlic
- 1 tsp red chili chopped
- 2 tbsp butter
- ½ cup bread crumbs
- 2 tbsp cilantro chopped

**Method**

Sauté the garlic and shallot in the butter for a minute or two.

Add the rest ingredients and mix without the lime and oysters.

Spread the crumble over the oyster and place them on a grill.

Allow it to cook until sizzling and brown.

Serve with lemon slices.

# Choi Steamed Buns

We see Ryan taking charge of star lab in the movie; the buns are a great way to celebrate.

**Cook time 90 minutes**

**Makes about 18 buns**

**Ingredients**

- 350g plain flour
- 1 sachet of yeast about 2 ½ tsp
- 1 cup of warm milk
- 1/8 cup sugar

**Method**

Proof yeast in milk and sugar.

Add flour to form the dough, and allow it to rest.

Flatten out dough and roll into a log shape.

Cut into size and place in a steamer.

Cook until puffed and soft.

Serve as desired.

# Cocoa with Martha

After the death of Superman, Lois and Martha meet up for the first time over a hot mug of cocoa (sounds right).

**Prep time 30 minutes**

**Serves 2**

## Ingredients

- 1/3 cup unsweetened cocoa powder
- 3 cups non-fat milk powder
- 2 tbsp honey or more
- ¼ tsp sea salt
- A dash of cayenne for kick
- Hot water to mix

## Method

Add the ingredients into mugs.

Add the piping hot water and stir.

Enjoy.

# Gold Mashed Yukon Gold Potatoes

A little gold on wonder woman, this mash is as smooth and sleek as her.

**Cook time 35 minutes**

**Serves 4**

**Ingredients**

- 1 ½ pound Yukon gold potatoes, peeled and cut into cubes
- 1 ¼ cups heavy cream
- 4 tbsp butter
- 1 tbsp chopped scallions
- Salt and pepper to taste

**Method**

Cook potatoes in a pressure cooker with salt until soft for about 20 minutes.

Drain the potatoes and pour into a mixer with the oval whip – reserve some of the water.

Start whipping.

Meanwhile, add 3 tbsp butter to a cream and bring to a simmer.

Gently add the mixture until a smooth and consistent mash is formed.

Add potato liquid if the mash is too thick.

Season and sprinkle scallions over.

Serve as desired with extra butter.

# The Heroes Spiced Meat

Long before avengers, heroes love the spice, and this recipe is delicious.

**Cook time 3 hours 15 minutes**

**Serves 2**

## Ingredients

- 2 large 1-inch thick rib-eye steaks
- 2 sprigs rosemary chopped
- 1 tsp garlic powder
- 1 tbsp smoked paprika
- 1 tsp cayenne
- ¼ cup light soy sauce
- ¼ cup canola oil
- Salt and black peppercorn

## Method

Mix all the ingredients to make a spice mix.

Apply generously over the steak and allow it to marinate for 2 hours.

In a cast-iron skillet, sear all sides and place in a 450 degrees F oven.

This should take 15 to 20 minutes or as your desire.

Serve as you want.

# Wonder Woman Shrimp Stir-Fry

This recipe takes inspiration from Wonder Woman's shield. It looks like a wok and this is a dish cooked and enjoyed in one.

**Cook time 15 minutes**

**Serves 2**

## Ingredients

- 1 dozen shrimps, peeled, deveined, and cleaned
- 1/3 cup vegetable broth
- 1 tbsp light soy sauce
- 1 tbsp oyster sauce
- 1 red bell pepper diced
- 1 red chili chopped
- 12 sugar snap peas
- ¼ cup oil
- 1 tsp garlic grated
- A dash of brown sugar
- 1 tsp corn starch
- ½ cup carrots

## Method

Mix the broth, soy sauce, oyster, sugar, corn starch in a bowl and set aide

Add the oil to the wok, stir fry the garlic, carrots, and peppers

Add the shrimps and pour the sauce over on low heat

Cook until shrimps are no longer translucent

Serve with any grain of choice

# A college kid sandwich

Cyborg is actually a college student, and what is the best meal for a student than sandwiches.

**Cook time 20 minutes**

**Serves 2**

## Ingredients

- 8 bacon rations
- 2 large eggs
- 3 heirloom tomatoes sliced
- 1 firm-ripe avocado sliced
- 4 iceberg lettuce leaves
- 2 tbsp chipotle mayo
- 4 bread slices

## Method

Crisp the bacon in a pan and set aside.

Slather 1 tbsp of mayo over both ends of the bread slice.

Layer the bacon, tomatoes, avocado, lettuce, and the other slice.

Serve.

# Aquaman Baked Scallops

They are simple and won't take up so much of your time.

**Cook time 25 minutes**

**Serves 3 – 4**

## Ingredients

- 15 large scallops, fresh and cleaned
- ½ tsp paprika, cayenne
- ½ tbsp lemon zest
- ½ cup panko crumbs
- ¼ cup grated parmesan
- Salt and pepper
- 2 tbsp chopped tarragon
- ½ stick butter
- 1 tbsp olive oil

## Method

Combine all the ingredients except the scallops in a bowl.

Arrange the scallop on a baking tray and cover with the crumb mix.

Cook in the oven for 12 -15 minutes.

# Flash's Healthy drink

Flash is seen performing some yoga moves, and this is the perfect way to start a fight or day.

**Prep time 10 minutes**

**Serves 2**

**Ingredients**

- 2 large bananas ripe
- 1 cup Greek yogurt
- ½ cup coconut milk or any of choice
- 3 – 6 ice cubes
- 1 tbsp honey
- A dash of cinnamon
- A sprinkle of cayenne

**Method**

Blend all the ingredients in a blender.

Pour into the glasses.

Enjoy.

# Barry's Pizza Box

He is the Flash, now recruited into the justice league. The scene shows him following Bruce into his car eating a pizza.

**Cook time 90 minutes**

**Serves 4**

## Ingredients

- 1 store-bought pizza dough
- An 8-inch oven-safe pan
- 4 ounces tomato sauce
- 1 tsp freshly chopped basil and spinach
- 2 cups mozzarella cheese
- Choose desired toppings
- 1 tbsp butter

## Method

Brush the pan with butter.

Spread the dough from edge to edge.

Spread the tomato sauce, add the toppings you chose.

Add the veggies.

Sprinkle generously with cheese.

Bake until crisp at the edges.

Serve.

# Flash Hotdog Scene

He saves the girl that would become his future partner from being pressed by a truck, and we see hotdogs flying around.

**Cook time 60 minutes**

**Makes 12**

## Ingredients

- 2 cups caramelized onion
- 400g beef ground
- 100g pork ground with fat
- 2 eggs
- 1 tsp black and white pepper each
- 1 tsp paprika
- ¼ tsp cumin & coriander
- Salt to taste
- ¼ cup cold milk
- The casing

## Method

Add all the ingredients to a bowl and mix well.

Place in a sausage stuffer and fix the casing at the base.

Gradually fill the casing and cook as desired.

Freeze any leftovers.

# Three is the magic number Cookies

The movie ends with the three boxes destroyed and Steppenwolf killed by Superman, Aquaman, and Wonder Woman.

**Cook time 50 minutes**

**Makes 2 dozen mini cookies**

## Ingredients

- 1 cup frozen butter cubes
- ½ cup baker's sugar
- 2¼ cups plain flour

## Method

Cream sugar and butter until fluffy.

Add the flour – might not be all.

Wrap and freeze.

Cut into shapes and bakes.

This is a great way to celebrate the victory for the league.

# Conclusion

Zack Snyder pulled out all the stops and took action and cinematography to a whole new level. The movie sees a better cohesion between the characters and a united front to destroy the earth's enemies. We cannot wait to see what will happen with Darkseid.

However, these recipes should get you started and enable you to watch this 4-hours long movie without any hunger pangs.

# About the Author

Luke Sack knew he wanted to be a chef from the tender age of 8 while helping his grandmother cook for his large family. The elderly matriarch taught him the beauty of a well-spiced meal and how even simple ingredients can be brought to life with the right seasonings. His grandmother had a huge impact on his life, so everything in his e-books is dedicated to her. She passed away shortly after he left for the Escoffier Culinary Arts School in Omaha, Nebraska and he always held her valuable lessons in his work and his heart.

Today, Luke lives with his family in Lincoln, Nebraska not far from his old home he shared with his grandmother. He is passing on the gift of culinary arts to his own children and instilling in them the same appreciation for simple meals seasoned to perfection. He runs a thriving cooking school with his wife, whom he met at Escoffier. Luke's cooking school teaches techniques ranging from simple baked chicken to the most complex recipes in haute cuisine.

Stay tuned for more culinary delights from Luke Sack as he expects to release more cooking e-books filled with recipes that you will adore!

# Author's Afterthoughts

**THANK YOU!** *thank you!*

Readers like you are the reason I get up in the morning! I am delighted that you decided to buy and read my book. Thank you for making a choice to get creative and healthier in the kitchen. I poured my heart into each and every page and my hope is you get the same fulfillment out of reading them.

With a multitude of books out there that offer this content, I am humbled and grateful that you decided to choose mine.

I thrive on constructive feedback, so please tell me what you thought of the book. Your opinions give me food for thought and your ideas help me move forward. Please leave a review on Amazon.com and let me know what you think.

Thank you,

Luke Sack

Printed in Great Britain
by Amazon